Mango Goes...

By Shaun Cornfoot & Jenny Leonard

When was the last time you went on an adventure?

The world is a big place filled with millions of people. Flowing rivers meander through thick rainforests, snow topped mountains rise up through the clouds and great cities sprawl like a concrete canvas.

In a far corner of the world there was a great ice plain.

Bright white snow stretched as far as the eye could see. Crystal blue sea merged with the sky above. At night, the sky filled with glistening stars. The ice plain was completely silent, apart from the gentle lapping of waves against the shore. At the edge of the ice plain was a small ice house.

Mango lived in the ice house on her own.

Every day she got up, went out fishing and returned home with her catch to make fish stew. Inside her ice house lopsided shelves creaked under the weight of a collection of colourful jars.

Peculiar maps hung from the walls of her ice house, showing the many different lands that make up the Earth. Mango was curious for what lay beyond the seas that surrounded her.

She wanted to feel the sensation of sand between her toes and the warm sun upon her face. But she didn't want to leave the comfort of her icy home with its warm glow and familiar walls.

One day, Mango awoke to a loud cracking sound. She jumped out of bed and hurried outside. To her surprise, a huge crack had appeared between her ice house and the mainland.

Suddenly, with a deafening snap, the ice house broke free and began to drift away. There was nothing she could do but watch, helplessly, as the ice plain where she had lived her whole life, faded into the distance.

Mango sat back, exhausted.
As the sun set she bobbed out into the vast expanse of water beyond.

After a long while drifting over the waves Mango spotted something breaking
through the top of the water. At first she was unsure what it was,
then quite suddenly three blinking eyes emerged and stared
directly at her. Slowly the stalks extended
upwards and the body of a large sea
creature came into full view.
It seemed to struggle
to balance itself
above the
water...

Upon settling on the surface of the water the creature spoke in a booming voice

"Hellooooo. My name is Reggie. What is your name small person? And why are you sailing in these dangerous waters? You never know the kind of mischief you might find yourself getting into swimming about these parts"

Mango was reassured by Reggie's friendly introduction. She was also in need of assistance, so she called back

"Hello Reggie, pleased to meet you. My name is Mango. Can you help me? I'm lost and I'm trying to find my way back home"

Reggie looked puzzled at first but then scooped his body to the edge of the ice house and gripped on. He lowered one of his eyes so it was directly in line with Mango's face

"Lost, you say? Where have you come from may I ask?"

Mango pointed vaguely out to the horizon

"I'm from the great ice plain over there...or maybe it's over there... or perhaps there?" she paused "To be honest, I don't know where I am or where I've come from"

"Never fear, little Mango, I think I can be of service"
He pushed his great tail under the water and propelled them both through the sea.
They laughed as they flew through the water together at such a speed.

Huge sploshes of sea whipped up at them.
It was the world's greatest rollercoaster!

The ice was shrinking fast and just before it disappeared Reggie abruptly stopped swimming. He raised his outside fin and pointed to the horizon. Mango looked in the direction that Reggie was pointing and could make out a faint blip, as the sea met the sky.

"This is where I leave you my intrepid explorer. I am sorry that I have been unable to help you back to your homeland but the land beyond should provide all you need. I wish you the best of luck with your journey home"

Reggie sunk back into the depths and Mango realised that she would have to continue on her own.

The blip on the horizon
was small at first but
gradually grew taller as
she bobbed towards it.

Soon it became an
island, filled with thick
vines and a sprawling
rainforest, surrounded by
a narrow strip of bright,
white sand.

As Mango drew closer to the island her ice house began to melt at an alarming rate. She paddled and rocked herself towards the land on the last piece of ice, until she washed up on the shore.
The heat was unbearable, especially in her thick coat.

Mango sat up and stared out to sea, wondering what to do next. She was lost and her house had just melted in front of her eyes.

This hot and humid island felt a million miles from the ice plain she called home.

Suddenly she heard a rustling in the trees behind her. Out of nowhere a figure emerged, crashing through the undergrowth and skidding to a halt directly in front of her.

Mango lurched backwards, startled at the unexpected arrival of this strange being. He had a long grey beard that tumbled all the way down to his belly button. Wisps of silver, black and white wiry hair weaved through his matted locks. His skin was brown, leathery and creased. His left eye bulged and looked directly at Mango. His right eye stared absentmindedly into the distance.

Surveying Mango, he pondered how and why this strange little intruder had arrived on his island. As he looked he broke into a wide smile exposing rows of yellowed teeth that stuck out like a broken picket fence.

He cleared his throat and said, in an unexpectedly high voice

Hello little girl
And how do you do?
Are you here for a while
Or just passing through?

Although Mango was a little scared, she knew that it was rude to not respond to a question. She stood up straight, wiped the hair back from her sweaty brow and introduced herself with as much confidence as she could muster...

"Hello Sir. My name is Mango. I am from an ice plain many miles from this island. My house broke from the mainland and I floated away.

A kind sea creature pushed me to the shore and my house melted away on the beach. I'm not s-s-scared though, honestly I'm not!"

Mango stuttered a little.

The old man let out a sharp chuckle, rolled his right eye to the sky and stroked his long beard. He thrust his hand toward Mango's. The skin on his right hand was creased and gnarled, like bark from an old tree. His nails were long and ragged.

Mango extended her hand and shook his.

The man spoke, more gently this time...

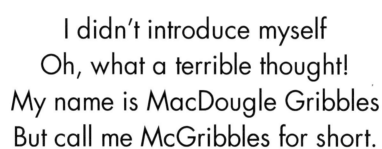

Nice to meet you Mango
And welcome to my home.
I've lived here for a hundred years
And always on my own.

I didn't introduce myself
Oh, what a terrible thought!
My name is MacDougle Gribbles
But call me McGribbles for short.

You've travelled far across the waves
And hungry you must be.
Shall we find you some delicious fruit
Up there in the canopy?

McGribbles turned his back and darted into the bush. His long spidery legs sprinted ahead though the undergrowth.

His strides were triple the size of Mango's!

Mango tore her way through spider webs, scrambled over boulders and waded through narrow streams. McGribbles was calling back but her thick coat was weighing her down.

She was puffing and panting like an old steam train.

Finally, they reached a group of unusual trees.
McGribbles turned to Mango and motioned upwards...

To reach the fruit we have to climb
From the trunk, to the top of the tree.
Just use the steps on this sand tower
And quickly follow me.

Mango looked at the bizarre sand structure. Driftwood steps spiralled up to the sky.
Quick as a flash, McGribbles jumped and clung onto the first step like a monkey.
He shimmied his body swiftly up the sand tower from step to step
and beckoned Mango to follow.

To Mango's surprise, the steps were sturdy and
she was able to work her way up easily.

As she reached the top she spotted
McGribbles. He was sitting on the tallest
branch dangling his skinny legs over the edge.

He stretched his hand down to hers
and hauled her up onto the branch.

Upon finding her balance Mango inspected her surroundings. At the end of every branch hung a plump, oval shaped fruit.

She turned to McGribbles

"What are these things called?"

The fruit is called a Mango
And it looks just like you!
Here, take this piece and taste it
It's much nicer than fish stew!

Mango bit into the soft flesh of the fruit.
Her cheeks exploded with the sweetness of
tasty juice. She turned to McGribbles

"WOW! This *is* the most delicious food I have
ever eaten"

The scent rose up through her nose and made
her smile with fruit-stained teeth.

Mango perched next to McGribbles and looked out over the horizon. The sun was beginning to set and it cast a dark orange glow across the shimmering waves in the distance.

They stared out towards the sea. Mango spoke quietly to McGribbles...

"Thank you for finding me and teaching me how to climb the tallest tree and pick the ripest fruit. This has been the best day of my life. Before today I was too scared to leave my ice house. Maybe I can just stay here, with you, and eat Mango fruit every day?"

McGribbles tilted his head and looked out towards the dipping sun...

Ah my little Mango
You have so much more to see.
The world is such a wonderful place
Far away from this big tree.

I have travelled far and wide
I've seen every grain of sand.
Now it's time for your adventure
And I'll lend you a hand.

First of all just get some rest
Before you start your trip.
Lay down and get some sleep now
And I shall make your ship.

McGribbles sprang up, swung off the branch and disappeared.

Mango lay down and looked up at the night sky. She wanted to stay on the island but she trusted the words of this wise old man.

Far above her shone a thousand million stars.

Her eyelids dropped once, then twice and she drifted off to sleep.

After what seemed like a minute,
a loud buzzing of insect noises awoke
Mango from her slumber.

McGribbles was nowhere to be seen,
so she decided to scramble out of the tree.

Across the beach she spotted a small wonky ship laying at edge of the waves.

Out of the corner of her eye Mango spotted McGribbles running
down the beach towards her. As he got closer he called out...

Go forth courageous Mango,
For wherever Mango goes
She shall be the lucky one
From her head down to her toes!

Mango hopped into the rickety boat as
McGribbles took hold of the back and pushed her
away from the shore.

As she turned back they exchanged big wide
grins and she called out

"I'll always remember you and the juiciest of all
fruits from this land!"

Mango had made a new friend, she had her very own ship and her adventure was just beginning...